101 Amazing Things to do with Money In Retirement

A Comprehensive Guide to Life After Work: Maximizing Your Finances and Enjoying Every Moment

Victor S. Jameson

Table of Contents

Introduction

Welcome to the adventure of a lifetime—your retirement. For years, you've dedicated your time and energy to work, family, and countless responsibilities. Now, it's time to embrace the golden years and live for yourself. This book is your guide to making the most of this incredible chapter, filled with possibilities, passions, and dreams long deferred.

Imagine waking up with the freedom to explore new hobbies, embark on thrilling adventures, or simply savor a quiet morning coffee. Retirement isn't just about slowing down; it's about rediscovering joy, finding new purpose, and experiencing life with the wisdom and grace you've earned.

Join me on a journey to unlock the full potential of your retirement. Together, we'll dive into exciting experiences, from skydiving to culinary escapades, and explore ways to give back to the community, ensuring every moment is rich with meaning and fulfillment. Let's turn this new chapter into your best one yet. Welcome to the adventure—welcome to your golden years.

Understanding Retirement: Embracing the Golden Years

Retirement is often viewed as the pinnacle of a long and fruitful career, a phase where one can finally reap the rewards of years of hard work. However, the transition to retirement is not just about ending employment; it's about beginning a new chapter in life. Embracing the golden years involves a multifaceted approach that encompasses emotional, physical, and financial readiness.

Emotionally, retirement can be a significant adjustment. Many people identify strongly with their professional roles, and stepping away can lead to a sense of loss or uncertainty about one's purpose. To counteract this, it's important to focus on the opportunities that retirement offers rather than what is being left behind. This could be the perfect time to explore passions that were previously sidelined due to work commitments. Engaging in hobbies, learning new skills, or even starting a new venture can provide a renewed sense of purpose and fulfillment.

Physically, maintaining health is paramount in retirement. Without the daily structure of a job, it can be easy to slip into sedentary habits. Embracing the golden years means taking proactive steps to stay active and healthy. Regular exercise, whether it's joining a fitness class, walking, swimming, or even gardening, can improve both physical and mental health. Additionally, routine medical check-ups and a balanced diet are crucial to sustaining long-term health and vitality.

Financial readiness is another critical component of a fulfilling retirement. Many retirees live on a fixed income, making it essential to have a clear understanding of finances. Creating a budget that accounts for regular expenses, healthcare costs, and leisure activities can help prevent financial stress. It's also beneficial to have an emergency fund for unexpected expenses.

Social connections play a vital role in embracing the golden years. Retirement can sometimes lead to feelings of isolation, especially if social interactions were primarily work-related. Joining clubs, volunteering, or participating in community activities can foster new friendships and keep social skills sharp. These interactions not only provide enjoyment but also contribute to emotional well-being.

Travel is another exciting aspect of retirement. With fewer obligations, retirees have the freedom to explore new destinations. Whether it's visiting family, discovering new cultures, or simply relaxing in a favorite spot, travel can enrich life and provide countless memorable experiences. Lastly, it's important to stay mentally active. Engaging in activities that challenge the brain, such as reading, puzzles, or even taking courses, can keep the mind sharp. Many retirees find joy in mentoring, sharing their wealth of knowledge and experience with younger generations.

Embracing the golden years is about finding a balance between relaxation and engagement, ensuring that each day is meaningful and enjoyable. By focusing on emotional, physical, financial, and social well-being, retirees can create a fulfilling and vibrant new chapter of life.

The Power of Financial Freedom: Making Your Money Work for You

Financial freedom is the cornerstone of a secure and enjoyable retirement. It's about having enough resources to live comfortably without the constant worry of running out of money. Achieving financial freedom requires careful planning, smart investments, and prudent management of resources.

One of the first steps to financial freedom in retirement is understanding your financial picture. This means having a clear idea of your assets, liabilities, income sources, and expenses. Retirement often brings a shift from earning a salary to relying on pensions, social security, savings, and investments. Ensuring these income streams are sufficient to cover your lifestyle is crucial.

Investing wisely is a key component of making your money work for you. Diversification is essential to minimize risk and maximize returns. This might involve a mix of stocks, bonds, real estate, and other investment vehicles. Consulting with a financial advisor can provide tailored advice to align your investments with your risk tolerance and retirement goals.

Passive income streams are another powerful tool for financial freedom. These are earnings derived from investments or businesses that do not require active involvement. Examples include dividends from stocks, rental income from property, or royalties from creative works. Passive income provides a steady cash flow, reducing reliance on savings.

Debt management is also critical. Entering retirement with significant debt can erode financial security. Paying down high-interest debt before retiring can free up more of your income for enjoyable activities and necessary expenses. In retirement, it's wise to avoid taking on new debt unless absolutely necessary.

Healthcare costs can be a significant concern in retirement. Having adequate health insurance, including long-term care coverage, can protect against substantial medical expenses that could deplete savings. Understanding what your insurance covers and budgeting for out-of-pocket expenses is essential for financial planning.

Estate planning ensures that your financial legacy is protected and distributed according to your wishes. This involves creating or updating wills, setting up trusts, and designating beneficiaries. Proper estate planning can also provide peace of mind knowing that your loved ones are taken care of.

Living within your means is fundamental to sustaining financial freedom. This involves creating a realistic budget that includes not just necessities but also allowances for leisure and unexpected costs. Regularly reviewing and adjusting this budget can help maintain financial health.

Lastly, continuous learning and adaptability in financial matters can significantly benefit retirees. Keeping informed about market trends, new investment opportunities, and changes in tax laws can help make informed decisions that enhance financial security.

Financial freedom in retirement is not just about having enough money; it's about managing and growing those resources wisely to ensure a comfortable and worry-free life. By understanding your financial situation, investing smartly, managing debt, planning for healthcare, and staying informed, you can make your money work for you, providing the freedom to enjoy your retirement to the fullest.

1
Travel and Adventure

Wanderlust Wonders: Exploring the World in Retirement

Retirement opens up a world of possibilities, and for many, the prospect of travel is one of the most exciting. With fewer commitments and more free time, retirees can explore the globe, immerse themselves in different cultures, and experience the wonders they may have only dreamed about during their working years. Wanderlust can take retirees to iconic landmarks, vibrant cities, and serene natural landscapes, making travel an enriching and fulfilling aspect of retirement.

One of the first steps in planning travel during retirement is creating a travel bucket list. This list should include destinations that hold personal significance, places that have always sparked curiosity, and new locales that promise unique experiences. Whether it's the ancient ruins of Machu Picchu, the bustling streets of Tokyo, or the breathtaking fjords of Norway, having a bucket list helps retirees prioritize their travel goals and map out their adventures.

Traveling in retirement also means having the luxury of time, allowing for extended stays in each destination. Instead of rushing through a city in a few days, retirees can spend weeks or even months exploring a region in depth. This slow travel approach enables a deeper connection with the local culture and environment. For instance, spending a month in Provence, France, allows for leisurely wine tours, daily market visits, and the chance to build relationships with locals.

Another significant advantage of retirement travel is the ability to choose the best times to visit popular destinations, avoiding peak tourist seasons. Traveling during the shoulder seasons—spring and fall—offers a more relaxed experience with fewer crowds and often lower prices. Visiting Italy in April or Greece in October, for example, can provide a more authentic and enjoyable travel experience.

Travel also offers retirees the opportunity to engage in lifelong learning. Many destinations provide educational tours, workshops, and cultural immersion programs. In cities like Florence or Barcelona, retirees can take art history courses that bring the rich cultural heritage to life. Language schools in places like Spain or Mexico offer immersive programs that enhance communication skills and deepen cultural understanding.

For those who crave adventure, retirement travel can include thrilling experiences such as trekking in the Himalayas, scuba diving in the Great Barrier Reef, or embarking on an African safari. These adventures not only provide adrenaline-pumping excitement but also create lasting memories and stories to share.

Moreover, group travel options like guided tours or cruises cater specifically to retirees, offering convenience and companionship. These tours handle the logistics, allowing travelers to focus on enjoying the journey. They also provide the chance to meet like-minded individuals and form new friendships.

Ultimately, exploring the world in retirement is about savoring the freedom to go where you want, when you want, and for as long as you desire. It's an opportunity to turn dreams into reality and discover the incredible beauty and diversity of our planet.

Off the Beaten Path: Unique Travel Experiences

While iconic landmarks and popular tourist destinations hold their charm, there is something incredibly special about venturing off the beaten path. For retirees looking to explore beyond the usual routes, unique travel experiences offer a richer and often more personal connection to the places they visit. These adventures take travelers to lesser-known destinations, providing a sense of discovery and exclusivity.

One of the most rewarding aspects of off-the-beaten-path travel is the chance to encounter unspoiled natural beauty. Hidden gems such as the Faroe Islands, with their dramatic cliffs and quaint villages, offer stunning landscapes without the crowds. Exploring the Patagonian wilderness in Argentina and Chile presents unparalleled opportunities for hiking, wildlife watching, and experiencing pristine natural environments.

Cultural immersion is another highlight of unique travel experiences. Visiting small, less-touristy towns allows retirees to engage more authentically with local traditions and lifestyles. For example, spending time in rural villages in Vietnam or Peru provides insight into daily life, from traditional cooking methods to age-old farming practices. Participating in local festivals or staying in homestays can offer an intimate understanding of the community and its culture. For those interested in history, off-the-beaten-path destinations often hold undiscovered treasures. Exploring the ancient ruins of Cappadocia in Turkey, with its cave dwellings and rock-hewn churches, provides a fascinating glimpse into a bygone era. The remote island of Socotra in Yemen, known for its unique biodiversity and ancient inscriptions, offers a rare combination of natural and historical wonders.

Adventure seekers will find plenty of excitement in lesser-known destinations. Sandboarding in the dunes of Namibia, diving in the untouched reefs of the Solomon Islands, or hiking the rugged terrain of Kyrgyzstan's Tien Shan mountains provides thrilling experiences far from the typical tourist trails. These adventures offer both physical challenges and the reward of discovering remote and beautiful parts of the world.

Food enthusiasts can also indulge in unique culinary experiences off the beaten path. Sampling local delicacies in the markets of Oaxaca, Mexico, or savoring the distinct flavors of Georgian cuisine in Tbilisi offers a culinary adventure that is both educational and delicious. Cooking classes, food tours, and visits to local farms can deepen the appreciation of a region's gastronomic heritage.

Retirees seeking tranquility and relaxation will find that off-the-beaten-path destinations often provide peaceful retreats. The serene beaches of the Azores, the quiet canals of the Mekong Delta, and the isolated temples of Bhutan offer respite from the hustle and bustle of more frequented sites. These tranquil settings are perfect for meditation, yoga, or simply unwinding in a beautiful and serene environment.

Ultimately, off-the-beaten-path travel experiences enrich retirement by providing unique, personal, and memorable adventures. They offer the chance to see the world from a different perspective, to connect deeply with new places and cultures, and to create stories that are truly one-of-a-kind.

Cruising into Retirement: Luxury Voyages and Exotic Destinations

Cruising offers retirees a luxurious and convenient way to explore multiple destinations while enjoying top-notch amenities and services. The allure of cruising lies in its combination of comfort, variety, and the ability to travel effortlessly from one exotic location to another. Whether it's sailing through the crystal-clear waters of the Caribbean, exploring the historic ports of the Mediterranean, or navigating the fjords of Norway, cruises provide a unique and enjoyable way to see the world.

Luxury cruises, in particular, cater to retirees looking for a premium travel experience. These voyages offer spacious and elegantly appointed cabins, gourmet dining options, and a range of onboard activities and entertainment. Many luxury cruise lines, such as Crystal Cruises, Regent Seven Seas, and Seabourn, provide all-inclusive packages that cover not only accommodation and meals but also shore excursions, gratuities, and even airfare in some cases. The convenience of cruising is a significant draw for retirees. Once on board, all the logistics are taken care of, allowing travelers to focus on relaxing and enjoying their journey. Cruises eliminate the need for constant packing and unpacking, as your comfortable cabin travels with you to each new destination. This makes cruising an especially appealing option for those who prefer a hassle-free travel experience.

Cruises offer a diverse range of destinations and itineraries, from tropical getaways to polar expeditions. A Caribbean cruise might include stops in the Bahamas, Jamaica, and St. Lucia, where passengers can enjoy beach excursions, snorkeling, and cultural tours. A Mediterranean cruise could take travelers to historic cities like Rome, Athens, and Istanbul, offering guided tours of ancient ruins, museums, and local markets.

For those seeking more exotic adventures, expedition cruises provide access to remote and less-traveled regions. These voyages often feature smaller ships designed to navigate narrow waterways and reach isolated destinations. An expedition cruise to Antarctica, for example, offers the chance to witness breathtaking icebergs, observe penguin colonies, and enjoy guided excursions led by expert naturalists. Similarly, a river cruise on the Amazon allows for close encounters with diverse wildlife and visits to indigenous communities.

In addition to exploring new destinations, cruises offer a wealth of onboard activities to keep retirees entertained and engaged. From cooking classes and wine tastings to fitness centers and spa treatments, there is something for everyone. Enrichment programs, such as guest lectures, art classes, and language courses, provide opportunities for learning and personal growth.

Cruises also offer a social aspect that many retirees appreciate. With a variety of lounges, dining venues, and group activities, cruises provide ample opportunities to meet and connect with fellow travelers. This can lead to new friendships and shared experiences that enhance the overall enjoyment of the journey.

Safety and health considerations are also well-addressed on luxury cruises. High standards of cleanliness, medical facilities on board, and well-trained staff ensure that passengers can travel with peace of mind. Many cruise lines have implemented enhanced health protocols to safeguard against illnesses, making cruising a safe option for retirees. Ultimately, cruising into retirement offers a perfect blend of adventure, luxury, and convenience. Whether exploring familiar destinations or venturing into the unknown, cruises provide a comfortable and enjoyable way to see the world. With their diverse itineraries, exceptional amenities, and opportunities for social interaction, cruises ensure that retirees can make the most of their golden years, creating lasting memories along the way.

2

Leisure and Lifestyle

Pursuing Passions: Investing in Hobbies and Interests

Retirement offers the perfect opportunity to dive deep into passions and hobbies that may have taken a backseat during one's working years. With more free time and often more disposable income, retirees can explore interests that bring joy, satisfaction, and a sense of purpose. Pursuing passions not only enriches life but also contributes to mental and physical well-being.

Art and Craftsmanship

For those with a creative flair, investing in art supplies or setting up a personal studio can be immensely rewarding. Whether it's painting, sculpting, pottery, or woodworking, engaging in artistic activities can provide a profound sense of accomplishment. Many retirees find joy in creating pieces of art that express their inner thoughts and emotions. Additionally, taking classes or joining art groups can enhance skills and provide social interaction.

Gardening

Gardening is another hobby that offers both physical activity and mental relaxation. Retirees can transform their yards into beautiful, personalized landscapes or cultivate a vegetable garden that supplies fresh, organic produce. Gardening requires knowledge of plants, soil, and weather conditions, making it an intellectually stimulating pursuit. Furthermore, the act of nurturing plants and watching them grow can be deeply fulfilling.

Music and Performing Arts

Music can be a powerful passion, whether it involves learning a new instrument, joining a choir, or simply enjoying regular concerts and performances. Retirees with a love for music might invest in a high-quality instrument or sound system to enhance their experience. Those inclined towards the performing arts can participate in local theater productions, dance classes, or even start a small community band or ensemble. Engaging in music and performance not only provides joy but also sharpens cognitive skills and enhances emotional health.

Collecting

Collecting can be a fascinating and rewarding hobby. Whether it's stamps, coins, antiques, or rare books, building a collection involves research, patience, and often, a bit of treasure hunting. Retirees can attend auctions, visit flea markets, or travel to specialty stores to find unique items for their collections. Sharing their collections with others, either through exhibitions or informal gatherings, can also be a source of pride and social interaction.

Writing and Literature

For those who love words, retirement is an ideal time to write that novel, memoir, or collection of poetry. Investing in a good writing space, perhaps a cozy study with all the necessary tools, can create an inspiring environment. Joining writers' groups or attending literary festivals can provide feedback and foster connections with fellow writers. Reading, too, remains a timeless hobby, and retirees can invest in a home library, filled with classic literature, contemporary works, or specialized collections.

Sports and Physical Activities

Staying active is crucial in retirement, and pursuing sports can be both enjoyable and beneficial for health. Retirees might take up golf, tennis, swimming, or hiking. Investing in quality sports equipment or club memberships can enhance the experience. Participating in sports not only keeps the body fit but also provides opportunities to meet new people and engage in friendly competition.

Travel as a Hobby

For many, travel becomes a passionate hobby in retirement. Retirees can delve into the rich histories, cultures, and landscapes of various destinations. They might join travel clubs, attend travel seminars, or invest in high-quality travel gear. Keeping a travel journal or starting a travel blog can also be a fulfilling way to document and share adventures. Pursuing passions in retirement is about more than just passing the time; it's about enriching life, discovering new talents, and staying mentally and physically active. By investing in hobbies and interests, retirees can create a vibrant, fulfilling retirement experience.

Creating Your Dream Sanctuary: Home Renovations and Luxuries

Retirement is the perfect time to transform your home into a personal sanctuary, a place that reflects your tastes and provides comfort and luxury. With the freedom to invest in home improvements, retirees can create spaces that cater to relaxation, hobbies, and entertaining friends and family. Home renovations not only enhance the quality of life but also increase the property's value.

Redesigning Living Spaces

One of the most impactful renovations is redesigning the living spaces. This could involve knocking down walls to create an open-plan living area, installing large windows for more natural light, or upgrading furniture to ensure comfort and style. Investing in high-quality, comfortable seating and entertainment systems can turn the living room into a central hub for relaxation and socializing.

Kitchen Upgrades

For many, the kitchen is the heart of the home, and upgrading this space can greatly enhance daily living. Modernizing the kitchen with state-of-the-art appliances, custom cabinetry, and high-end countertops can make cooking and entertaining more enjoyable. Adding a kitchen island with seating provides a social focal point where family and friends can gather. Smart kitchen technology, such as programmable ovens and refrigerators with built-in screens, can add convenience and efficiency.

Bathroom Luxuries

Bathrooms are another key area for renovation. Turning a standard bathroom into a spa-like retreat can involve installing features such as walk-in showers with rainfall showerheads, soaking tubs, heated floors, and high-end fixtures. Adding elements like towel warmers, soft lighting, and high-quality tiles can create a serene and luxurious atmosphere.

Outdoor Living

Creating a beautiful and functional outdoor living space can significantly enhance the enjoyment of your home. This might include building a deck or patio, installing an outdoor kitchen, or creating a cozy fire pit area. Landscaping with lush gardens, water features, and comfortable outdoor furniture can transform a backyard into an oasis for relaxation and entertainment. Investing in a pool or hot tub can provide both leisure and a focal point for gatherings.

Home Office or Studio

For retirees pursuing new hobbies or working on projects, having a dedicated home office or studio is essential. This space can be tailored to specific needs, whether it's a quiet study for writing, a studio for art, or a workshop for crafting. High-quality lighting, comfortable furnishings, and ample storage are key components of an effective and inspiring workspace.

Bedrooms

Creating a tranquil and luxurious bedroom can significantly improve quality of life. Investing in a high-quality mattress and bedding, blackout curtains, and calming décor can enhance sleep and relaxation. Adding amenities like a reading nook, a walk-in closet, or an en-suite bathroom can make the bedroom a true sanctuary.

Smart Home Technology

Incorporating smart home technology can add convenience and security. Automated lighting, climate control, and security systems can be controlled via smartphones or voice commands. Smart home systems can also include energy-efficient solutions like programmable thermostats and solar panels, which can reduce costs and environmental impact.

Personal Touches

Finally, adding personal touches to the home ensures it reflects your personality and style. This could involve displaying cherished artwork, family photos, or travel souvenirs. Custom-built furniture or bespoke design elements can also add uniqueness and character to the space.

Creating your dream sanctuary in retirement is about making your home a place of comfort, luxury, and personal expression. Thoughtful renovations and investments in high-quality amenities can transform your living environment, making it a true reflection of your tastes and a haven for relaxation and enjoyment.

Epicurean Escapades: Culinary Adventures and Fine Dining

Retirement offers the perfect opportunity to embark on epicurean adventures, exploring the world of food and drink with newfound leisure and curiosity. From experimenting in your kitchen to dining at the finest restaurants, culinary pursuits can provide immense pleasure and satisfaction. Engaging with food on a deeper level not only delights the senses but also offers a way to connect with different cultures and traditions.

Home Cooking and Baking

For those who love to cook, retirement is the ideal time to delve deeper into the culinary arts. Investing in high-quality kitchen tools and appliances can elevate the cooking experience. Retirees can explore new recipes, perfect their baking skills, or even take online cooking classes to learn new techniques. Creating gourmet meals at home not only provides a sense of accomplishment but also allows for healthier eating and creative expression.

Gardening and Farm-to-Table

Many retirees find joy in growing their own fruits, vegetables, and herbs. A home garden or even a few potted plants can provide fresh ingredients for delicious, home-cooked meals. The farm-to-table movement emphasizes using locally sourced and homegrown produce, which can enhance the flavor and nutritional value of meals. Gardening also provides physical activity and a deeper connection to the food on your plate.

Wine and Spirits

Exploring the world of wine and spirits can be a delightful hobby. Retirees might invest in building a wine cellar or take trips to renowned wine regions like Napa Valley, Bordeaux, or Tuscany. Tasting and learning about different wines, understanding the art of pairing wine with food, and even trying your hand at making homemade wine can be enriching experiences. Similarly, exploring craft beers, distilleries, and the art of cocktail making can add another dimension to culinary adventures.

Cooking Classes and Workshops

Taking cooking classes, whether in person or online, can expand culinary horizons. Many cities offer gourmet cooking schools where retirees can learn from professional chefs. Workshops on specific cuisines, such as Thai, Italian, or Japanese, provide hands-on experience and deepen cultural appreciation. Participating in cooking vacations or culinary tours can combine travel and learning, offering immersive experiences in places like France, Mexico, or India.

Gourmet Food Clubs and Subscriptions

Subscribing to gourmet food clubs or meal kit services can introduce retirees to new ingredients and recipes. These services deliver high-quality, unique, and often hard-to-find foods right to your doorstep. Trying out different cheeses, charcuterie, or international delicacies can make for exciting culinary explorations at home.

Fine Dining Experiences

Retirement is also the time to indulge in fine dining experiences. Visiting Michelin-starred restaurants, renowned for their exquisite cuisine and exceptional service, can be a highlight. Many top restaurants offer tasting menus that showcase the chef's creativity and expertise. Fine dining provides not only a culinary treat but also an opportunity to appreciate the artistry and dedication that goes into each dish.

Food Festivals and Farmers' Markets

Food festivals and farmers' markets offer retirees an exciting way to explore local and international cuisine. These events celebrate the richness of culinary traditions and provide an opportunity to taste a variety of dishes in one place. Attending food festivals, whether it's a seafood festival in Maine, a chili cook-off in Texas, or a wine and food festival in Italy, can be a delightful experience. These festivals often feature cooking demonstrations, tastings, and workshops that provide a deeper understanding of different culinary practices.

Farmers' markets, on the other hand, offer fresh, local produce and artisanal goods. Visiting these markets can become a weekly tradition, where retirees can buy fresh ingredients, meet local farmers, and discover new products. The direct interaction with producers adds a personal touch to shopping, and the high quality of fresh produce can inspire new cooking ventures at home.

Culinary Tours and Travel

Culinary tours combine the love of travel with the excitement of food discovery. These tours take retirees to the heart of culinary regions, offering an immersive experience that goes beyond dining. In Italy, for example, culinary tours might include visits to vineyards, olive oil tastings, and hands-on pasta-making classes. In Japan, food tours can offer insights into sushi preparation, sake brewing, and traditional tea ceremonies.

Exploring street food is another thrilling aspect of culinary travel. Cities like Bangkok, Marrakech, and Mexico City are renowned for their vibrant street food scenes. Sampling local street food not only provides an authentic taste of the culture but also supports local vendors and small businesses.

Food Writing and Blogging

For retirees with a passion for both food and writing, starting a food blog or writing a cookbook can be a fulfilling project. Documenting culinary adventures, sharing recipes, and reviewing restaurants can connect retirees with a broader community of food enthusiasts. Blogging platforms and social media provide easy ways to share experiences and build an audience. Writing a cookbook allows retirees to compile favorite recipes and culinary stories, potentially leaving a legacy for family and friends. Whether self-published or pursued through traditional publishing routes, creating a cookbook can be a rewarding way to celebrate a lifelong love of food.

Private Dining and Supper Clubs

Creating a private dining experience at home or joining a supper club can bring fine dining to a more intimate setting. Retirees can host themed dinner parties, inviting friends and family to enjoy a curated menu paired with fine wines. These events can range from casual gatherings to elaborate, multi-course meals.

Joining or forming a supper club can also provide regular opportunities to share meals with a group of like-minded food lovers. These clubs often rotate hosting duties among members, allowing each person to showcase their culinary skills and introduce new dishes to the group.

Volunteering and Culinary Philanthropy

For retirees looking to give back, volunteering with food-related charities can be a meaningful way to combine a passion for food with community service. Organizations such as food banks, soup kitchens, and community gardens often seek volunteers to help with various tasks, from preparing meals to organizing food drives.

Culinary philanthropy can also involve supporting initiatives that address food insecurity and promote sustainable agriculture. Retirees might choose to donate to causes that provide meals for those in need, support local farmers, or promote healthy eating habits in schools. Retirement opens up a world of possibilities for culinary adventures and fine dining. From home cooking and gardening to gourmet dining and food festivals, the pursuit of epicurean escapades can bring immense joy and satisfaction. By exploring different cuisines, investing in quality ingredients and kitchen tools, and sharing culinary experiences with others, retirees can savor the many flavors of life. Whether through travel, education, or community involvement, the culinary journey in retirement can be as rich and rewarding as the dishes themselves.

3

Luxury and Exclusivity

Living the High Life: Indulging in Luxury Experiences

Retirement is a time when many individuals seek to reward themselves for years of hard work by indulging in luxury experiences. Living the high life can encompass a variety of extravagant activities and pampering services that cater to comfort, elegance, and exclusivity. From high-end travel to exclusive memberships, these experiences offer unparalleled enjoyment and a chance to savor the finer things in life.

Luxury Travel

One of the most popular ways to indulge in luxury is through high-end travel. Staying at five-star hotels and resorts, where personalized service and opulent amenities are standard, can transform any trip into a lavish retreat. Iconic destinations like the Maldives, Bora Bora, and the Amalfi Coast are known for their exclusive resorts and breathtaking surroundings. Many luxury hotels offer private villas, butler services, and gourmet dining, ensuring a memorable stay.

Traveling in first-class or private jets enhances the journey itself, making long flights comfortable and enjoyable. The opulence of first-class cabins, with lie-flat seats, gourmet meals, and personalized service, sets the tone for a luxurious adventure from the moment you board.

Exclusive Dining Experiences

Fine dining at Michelin-starred restaurants provides an unforgettable culinary adventure. These restaurants are celebrated for their exceptional cuisine, creativity, and impeccable service. Tasting menus curated by world-renowned chefs offer a journey through multiple courses, each dish crafted to perfection. Private dining rooms within these establishments can provide an intimate setting for special occasions.

Beyond traditional fine dining, unique experiences such as private chef services or dining at chef's tables offer exclusive access to culinary expertise. Retirees can hire top chefs to prepare personalized meals in their homes or arrange for private dining experiences where they can interact with the chef and learn about the creation of each dish.

Luxury Spas and Wellness Retreats

Indulging in luxury spa treatments and wellness retreats is another way to experience the high life. World-class spas offer an array of treatments, from massages and facials to holistic therapies like acupuncture and aromatherapy. Retreats in tranquil settings, such as the Swiss Alps or the islands of Thailand, provide comprehensive wellness programs that include yoga, meditation, and personalized health consultations. These experiences promote relaxation and rejuvenation, ensuring that retirees can enjoy their time with a renewed sense of vitality.

Exclusive Memberships and Clubs

Joining exclusive clubs can provide access to a host of luxury experiences. Private golf clubs, yacht clubs, and social clubs often offer luxurious amenities, including fine dining, exclusive events, and access to high-end facilities. These memberships provide a sense of community among like-minded individuals who share a taste for the finer things in life.

High-End Shopping

Indulging in luxury shopping is a beloved activity for many retirees. Shopping at high-end boutiques and flagship stores in fashion capitals like Paris, Milan, and New York offers a curated experience with personalized services. Personal shoppers and stylists can assist in selecting the finest clothing, accessories, and jewelry, ensuring that every purchase is a perfect addition to one's collection.

Private Concerts and Performances

Exclusive access to private concerts and performances offers a unique cultural experience. Hiring renowned musicians or attending intimate performances at private venues allows retirees to enjoy live music in an exclusive setting. Private boxes at opera houses or concert halls provide a luxurious way to enjoy world-class performances.

Adventure and Exploration

For those who seek adventure, luxury can also be found in high-end experiences like private safaris, yacht charters, and bespoke adventure tours. Private safaris in Africa, for instance, offer personalized itineraries, luxury accommodations, and the chance to explore wildlife with experienced guides. Chartering a yacht provides the freedom to explore remote islands and pristine waters, complete with a crew to cater to every need.

Living the high life in retirement means embracing luxury in every aspect of one's experiences. Whether through travel, dining, wellness, or exclusive memberships, these indulgences create unforgettable memories and elevate the retirement experience to extraordinary levels.

Collector's Corner: Investing in Fine Art, Jewelry, and Collectibles

Retirement can be the perfect time to delve into the world of fine art, jewelry, and collectibles. These investments not only offer financial benefits but also provide aesthetic pleasure and personal satisfaction. Collecting allows retirees to express their tastes, preserve cultural heritage, and potentially pass on valuable assets to future generations.

Fine Art

Investing in fine art is both a passion and a savvy financial strategy. Art pieces, whether they are paintings, sculptures, or photographs, can appreciate significantly over time. Retirees can explore galleries, art fairs, and auctions to discover works that resonate with them. Engaging with art consultants or advisors can provide insights into market trends and help identify promising artists.

Building a fine art collection involves more than just purchasing pieces; it requires an understanding of art history, styles, and the market. Retirees can take courses or attend lectures to deepen their knowledge. Displaying these works in one's home not only enhances the living space but also creates a personal gallery that reflects the collector's journey.

Jewelry

Investing in fine jewelry combines beauty with value. High-quality pieces, particularly those with rare gemstones or by renowned designers, can appreciate over time. Retirees can build a collection that includes classic pieces like diamond rings, sapphire necklaces, and pearl earrings, as well as contemporary designs that showcase craftsmanship and innovation.

Purchasing jewelry from reputable sources, understanding the value of different gemstones, and keeping abreast of market trends are essential for making informed investments. Additionally, attending jewelry shows and auctions can provide opportunities to acquire unique and valuable pieces. Proper care and storage of jewelry ensure that these investments remain in pristine condition.

Collectibles

Collectibles cover a wide range of items, from vintage cars and rare books to stamps and antique furniture. Each category offers its own set of challenges and rewards. Collecting requires patience, research, and often a network of fellow enthusiasts. Joining collector's clubs or associations can provide valuable connections and information.

Vintage cars, for instance, not only serve as investments but also offer the joy of ownership and the thrill of driving a piece of history. Attending car shows, auctions, and joining car clubs can enhance the collecting experience. Similarly, rare books provide a window into history and literature. Collectors might focus on first editions, signed copies, or works from specific periods or authors.

Stamps and coins are other popular collectibles that combine historical interest with potential value appreciation. Building a collection involves careful selection, authentication, and preservation. Collectors often enjoy the hunt for rare items and the satisfaction of completing a series or set.

Investment and Legacy

Investing in fine art, jewelry, and collectibles can also be a way to preserve wealth and create a legacy. These items can be passed down to heirs, providing both sentimental and financial value. It's essential to keep detailed records, including provenance, purchase details, and appraisals, to ensure the collection's value is well-documented.

Working with financial advisors who specialize in alternative investments can help retirees integrate their collections into a broader wealth management strategy. Insurance for valuable items is also crucial to protect against loss or damage.

The Ultimate Ride: Luxury Vehicles, Yachts, and Private Jets

For many retirees, indulging in luxury vehicles, yachts, and private jets represents the pinnacle of the high life. These modes of transportation offer unparalleled comfort, style, and freedom, making travel and exploration an extraordinary experience.

Luxury Vehicles

Owning a luxury car is a dream for many. Brands like Rolls-Royce, Bentley, and Aston Martin are synonymous with elegance and performance. These vehicles boast cutting-edge technology, exquisite craftsmanship, and powerful engines. Retirees can enjoy the thrill of driving a top-tier sports car or the comfort of a high-end sedan.

Collecting vintage and classic cars can also be a rewarding pursuit. Restoring and maintaining these vehicles not only preserves automotive history but also provides the satisfaction of owning a piece of engineering art. Car shows and rallies offer opportunities to showcase these treasures and connect with fellow enthusiasts.

Yachts

Yachting provides the ultimate in luxury and freedom on the water. Owning a yacht allows retirees to explore the world's most beautiful coastlines and remote islands at their own pace. Yachts come with a range of amenities, including spacious cabins, gourmet kitchens, and entertainment systems, ensuring a comfortable and opulent experience.

Chartering a yacht is an alternative that offers flexibility without the commitment of ownership. This option allows retirees to experience different yachts and explore various destinations. Many charters include a professional crew, providing personalized service and expert navigation.

Private Jets

Private jets epitomize convenience and luxury in air travel. Owning or chartering a private jet provides unparalleled flexibility, allowing retirees to travel according to their own schedules and preferences. Private jets offer luxurious interiors, state-of-the-art technology, and personalized service, ensuring a seamless and comfortable journey.

For those who frequently travel long distances or require flexibility, fractional ownership of a private jet can be a cost-effective solution. This arrangement allows for the benefits of private jet travel without the responsibilities of full ownership.

Living the high life in retirement is about embracing luxury in its many forms, whether through opulent experiences, sophisticated collections, or high-end transportation. Indulging in fine art, jewelry, and collectibles offers both aesthetic pleasure and financial benefits, while luxury vehicles, yachts, and private jets provide unmatched comfort and freedom. By exploring these avenues, retirees can create a lifestyle that celebrates their achievements and enriches their golden years with extraordinary experiences.

4

Giving Back and Making an Impact

Philanthropy in Retirement: Supporting Causes and Making a Difference

Philanthropy in retirement provides a meaningful way for retirees to use their time, resources, and skills to give back to society. It offers a sense of purpose and fulfillment by helping to address societal issues and supporting causes close to one's heart. Engaging in philanthropic activities can take many forms, from volunteering and direct donations to more structured approaches like establishing foundations and hosting fundraising events.

Volunteering Time and Expertise

Volunteering is one of the most hands-on ways retirees can make a difference. Many organizations, such as schools, hospitals, food banks, and shelters, rely heavily on volunteers. Retirees bring a wealth of experience and skills that can be invaluable. For example, retired teachers can tutor or mentor students, while those with business backgrounds can offer consulting to nonprofit organizations. Volunteering not only benefits the community but also keeps retirees active and socially engaged.

Direct Donations

Direct monetary donations are a straightforward and impactful way to support various causes. Retirees can contribute to local charities, national organizations, or international initiatives, depending on their interests. Researching and selecting reputable organizations ensures that donations are used effectively. Many retirees also opt to set up recurring donations to provide ongoing support, which helps organizations with long-term planning and sustainability.

Advocacy and Raising Awareness

Using one's voice to advocate for causes can amplify impact. Retirees can participate in awareness campaigns, write letters to policymakers, or use social media to highlight important issues. By leveraging their networks and platforms, retirees can bring attention to causes and influence positive change. Advocacy can be particularly powerful when combined with other philanthropic efforts, creating a comprehensive approach to making a difference.

Leaving a Legacy: Establishing Foundations and Scholarships

Establishing a foundation or scholarship is a profound way to create a lasting impact and leave a legacy that reflects one's values and passions. These initiatives can address specific needs, support long-term goals, and ensure continued support for causes important to the founder.

Establishing a Foundation

Creating a private foundation allows retirees to formalize their philanthropic efforts and have a structured approach to giving. Foundations can support a wide range of activities, from funding research and education to providing grants to other nonprofits. Setting up a foundation involves several steps:

1. **Define the Mission:**Clearly articulate the foundation's purpose and goals. This mission statement will guide all future activities and decisions.
2. **Legal Structure:** Choose the appropriate legal structure and register the foundation with the relevant authorities. This often involves creating a board of directors and developing bylaws.
3. **Funding:**Determine the initial funding and future funding strategies. This could include personal contributions, fundraising, or endowments.
4. **Grantmaking:** Establish criteria for selecting grant recipients and develop a process for evaluating and awarding grants.
5. **Management and Operations:** Hire staff or consultants to manage day-to-day operations, ensure compliance with regulations, and monitor the impact of funded projects.

Creating Scholarships

Scholarships are a powerful way to support education and open doors for future generations. Retirees can create scholarships at universities, colleges, or high schools to assist students with tuition, books, and other expenses. Steps to establish a scholarship include:

1. **Identify the Focus:** Decide on the criteria for the scholarship, such as academic achievement, financial need, field of study, or community service.
2. **Partner with an Institution:** Collaborate with an educational institution to manage the scholarship. Many schools have established processes for administering scholarships.
3. **Funding**: Determine the amount of the scholarship and whether it will be a one-time award or renewable. Set up an endowment if the scholarship is intended to be perpetual.
4. **Selection Process:**Develop a clear and fair selection process, often

involving an application, essay, and recommendations.

5. **Monitoring and Reporting:**Track the impact of the scholarship on recipients and report back to donors or stakeholders as needed.

Hosting Charity Galas and Fundraising Events

Charity galas and fundraising events are effective ways to raise funds and awareness for important causes. These events bring together donors, supporters, and community members in a festive and engaging environment. Successfully hosting such events requires careful planning, creativity, and attention to detail.

Planning the Event

1. **Define the Purpose**: Clearly outline the goals of the event, such as raising a specific amount of money, increasing awareness, or honoring donors and volunteers.

2. **Choose a Theme:** Select a theme that aligns with the cause and appeals to the target audience. A well-chosen theme can enhance the atmosphere and make the event memorable.

3. **Set a Budget:** Develop a detailed budget covering all aspects of the event, including venue rental, catering, entertainment, marketing, and administrative costs. Aim to maximize fundraising while keeping expenses reasonable.

Venue and Catering

Selecting the right venue is crucial to the success of the event. The venue should be accessible, appropriately sized, and align with the event's theme. Considerations include:

Capacity and Layout: Ensure the venue can comfortably accommodate the expected number of guests, with space for dining, entertainment, and socializing.

Location: Choose a location that is convenient for attendees, with ample parking or transportation options.

Ambiance: The venue should contribute to the event's atmosphere, whether it's an elegant ballroom, a modern gallery, or an outdoor garden.

Catering is another key element. Work with reputable caterers to design a menu that suits the event's theme and guest preferences. Offering a variety of food and drink options, including vegetarian and vegan choices, ensures all guests are satisfied.

Entertainment and Activities

Engaging entertainment can elevate the event and keep guests entertained. Options include live music, DJs, dance performances, or guest speakers. Interactive activities, such as auctions (silent or live), raffles, and photo booths, can also enhance the experience and boost fundraising efforts.

Live and Silent Auctions:Auctions can be a major fundraising component. Secure desirable items or experiences for guests to bid on, such as artwork, vacation packages, or exclusive experiences.
Guest Speakers: Invite influential figures or beneficiaries of the charity to speak about the cause, providing a personal touch and compelling narrative.

Marketing and Promotion

Effective promotion is essential to attract attendees and sponsors. Utilize a mix of marketing strategies, including:

Social Media: Leverage platforms like Facebook, Instagram, and Twitter to reach a broad audience. Create event pages, share updates, and engage with followers.
Email Campaigns: Send invitations and reminders to your mailing list. Personalize communications to highlight the importance of the event.
Press Releases:Issue press releases to local media outlets to generate coverage and build awareness.
Partnerships: Collaborate with local businesses or influencers to promote the event and reach new audiences.

Day-of Coordination and Follow-Up

On the day of the event, ensure smooth execution by having a detailed timeline and a team of volunteers or staff to manage various aspects. Assign specific roles and responsibilities, such as registration, auction management, and guest assistance.

After the event, follow up with attendees and donors to express gratitude and share the outcomes. Providing updates on how the funds will be used reinforces the impact of their contributions and encourages future support.

Philanthropy in retirement offers retirees a fulfilling way to give back and create a lasting impact. By supporting causes, establishing foundations and scholarships, and hosting charity events, retirees can make a significant difference in their communities and beyond. These activities not only address pressing needs but also provide a sense of purpose and legacy, ensuring that the retiree's contributions will be remembered and valued for years to come.

5 Wellness and Wellbeing

Rejuvenation Retreats: Spa Days and Wellness Getaways

Retirement offers the perfect opportunity to focus on personal well-being and rejuvenation. Rejuvenation retreats, encompassing spa days and wellness getaways, provide an idyllic setting for relaxation, self-care, and health enhancement. These retreats often combine luxurious pampering with holistic wellness practices, creating an environment where retirees can refresh their bodies and minds.

Spa Days

Spa days are an excellent way to experience relaxation and rejuvenation without committing to an extended stay. High-end spas offer a variety of treatments designed to pamper and revitalize. Common treatments include:

Massages: Techniques such as Swedish, deep tissue, hot stone, and aromatherapy massages help to relieve tension, improve circulation, and promote relaxation.

Facials: Customized facials address various skin concerns, leaving the skin refreshed and radiant. Options range from anti-aging treatments to hydrating and detoxifying facials.

Body Treatments: These treatments often include scrubs, wraps, and hydrotherapy, designed to exfoliate, hydrate, and detoxify the skin.

Manicures and Pedicures: These services not only beautify the nails but also include massages and moisturizing treatments for the hands and feet.

Many spas also offer amenities such as saunas, steam rooms, and relaxation lounges, enhancing the overall experience. Booking a spa day can be a solo retreat or a social activity with friends or family, providing both relaxation and a chance to connect.

Wellness Getaways

For a more immersive experience, wellness getaways offer extended retreats focused on holistic health and well-being. These retreats can vary in length from a weekend to several weeks and often take place in serene, picturesque locations. Key components of wellness getaways include:

Holistic Treatments: Beyond traditional spa services, wellness retreats often include acupuncture, reiki, and Ayurvedic treatments. These therapies aim to balance the body's energy and promote overall health.

Fitness Programs: Tailored fitness programs, including personal training, group classes, and guided outdoor activities, help participants stay active and improve their physical health.

Healthy Cuisine: Wellness retreats typically offer nutritious, gourmet meals designed to detoxify and nourish the body. Cooking classes and nutrition workshops are also common, providing skills that participants can take home.
Mind-Body Practices: Practices such as yoga, meditation, and mindfulness sessions are integral to wellness retreats, promoting mental clarity and emotional well-being.

Wellness getaways provide a holistic approach to health, addressing physical, mental, and emotional needs. Whether seeking a peaceful escape or a transformative experience, these retreats offer a sanctuary for rejuvenation.

Active Living: Fitness, Sports, and Adventure Activities

Staying active is crucial for maintaining health and vitality in retirement. Engaging in fitness, sports, and adventure activities not only keeps the body fit but also provides enjoyment and a sense of accomplishment. Active living can be tailored to individual preferences and fitness levels, ensuring that everyone can find an activity that suits them.

Fitness Programs

Structured fitness programs offer retirees a way to stay active under the guidance of professionals.

These programs can be found in gyms, community centers, and specialized fitness studios. Popular options include:

Aerobics and Cardio Classes: These classes improve cardiovascular health and endurance. Options range from low-impact aerobics to high-intensity interval training (HIIT).
Strength Training: Using weights, resistance bands, or bodyweight exercises, strength training helps maintain muscle mass, improve bone density, and enhance overall strength.
Flexibility and Balance Classes: Yoga, Pilates, and tai chi are excellent for improving flexibility, balance, and core strength. These practices also help prevent injuries and enhance mobility.

Sports

Participating in sports is a fun and social way to stay active. Many sports can be adapted to different fitness levels and provide both physical and mental benefits. Popular sports for retirees include:

Tennis and Pickleball: Both sports improve cardiovascular fitness, hand-eye coordination, and agility. Pickleball, in particular, is known for its easy-to-learn format and social nature.
Golf: Golf provides a moderate level of physical activity while promoting mental focus and relaxation. It's also a great way to enjoy the outdoors and socialize with friends.
Swimming: Swimming is a low-impact activity that works the entire body. It's

ideal for those with joint issues or those seeking a gentle yet effective workout.

Adventure Activities

For those who crave excitement, adventure activities offer thrilling ways to stay active and explore new experiences. Options for retirees include:

Hiking and Trekking: Exploring trails and nature preserves provides excellent cardiovascular exercise and an opportunity to connect with nature. Many hiking groups cater to different skill levels.
Cycling: Whether on road bikes, mountain bikes, or e-bikes, cycling is a versatile activity that can be enjoyed solo or in groups. It's great for building stamina and exploring scenic routes.
Kayaking and Canoeing: These water sports are not only great for upper body strength but also offer peaceful and scenic outdoor experiences. Many locations offer guided tours for beginners.

Mindfulness Matters: Meditation, Yoga, and Stress Relief

Retirement can bring a slower pace of life, but it also presents new challenges and adjustments. Incorporating mindfulness practices like meditation, yoga, and stress relief techniques can help retirees navigate these changes with grace and maintain mental and emotional well-being.

Meditation

Meditation is a powerful tool for cultivating inner peace and mental clarity. It involves focusing the mind and eliminating distractions, which can reduce stress and promote a sense of calm. Common meditation practices include:

Mindfulness Meditation: This practice involves paying attention to the present moment without judgment. It can be done sitting, lying down, or even walking.
Guided Meditation: Using recordings or apps, guided meditations lead participants through visualization and relaxation exercises, making it easier for beginners to start.
Transcendental Meditation: This technique uses a mantra—a specific word or sound—to help the mind settle into a state of restful alertness.

Regular meditation practice can improve concentration, reduce anxiety, and enhance overall well-being. Many community centers and wellness studios offer meditation classes or groups, providing a supportive environment for practice.

Yoga

Yoga combines physical postures, breathing exercises, and meditation to promote overall health. It's adaptable to all fitness levels and can be practiced in various styles:

Hatha Yoga: This gentle form of yoga focuses on basic postures and breathing techniques, making it ideal for beginners.
Vinyasa Yoga: Known for its fluid, dynamic sequences, vinyasa yoga provides a more vigorous workout and improves cardiovascular health.
Restorative Yoga: This practice uses props to support the body in passive poses, promoting deep relaxation and stress relief.

Regular yoga practice enhances flexibility, strength, and balance while also calming the mind. It's a holistic approach to health that benefits both body and mind.

Stress Relief Techniques

Managing stress is crucial for maintaining health and happiness in retirement. Stress relief techniques can be incorporated into daily routines to enhance relaxation and resilience:

Breathing Exercises: Techniques like deep breathing, diaphragmatic breathing, and alternate nostril breathing help calm the nervous system and reduce stress.

Progressive Muscle Relaxation: This involves tensing and relaxing different muscle groups to release tension and promote relaxation.
Mindfulness Practices: Mindfulness can be integrated into everyday activities, such as mindful eating, walking, or even chores, by focusing fully on the present moment.

Combining these practices creates a comprehensive approach to stress management, ensuring retirees can enjoy their time with greater peace and contentment.

Rejuvenation retreats, active living, and mindfulness practices offer retirees numerous ways to enhance their well-being and embrace a fulfilling lifestyle. Spa days and wellness getaways provide relaxation and holistic health benefits, while fitness, sports, and adventure activities keep the body active and engaged. Mindfulness practices, including meditation and yoga, support mental and emotional health, helping retirees navigate their golden years with serenity and vitality. By integrating these activities into their routine, retirees can enjoy a balanced, healthy, and joyful retirement.

6

Personal Growth and Development

Lifelong Learning: Education and Skill Development in Retirement

Retirement is an ideal time for lifelong learning and skill development. With more free time and fewer professional obligations, retirees can pursue educational opportunities and hobbies that may have been sidelined during their working years. Lifelong learning not only keeps the mind sharp but also provides a sense of achievement and purpose.

Continuing Education

Many retirees return to formal education to learn new subjects or deepen their knowledge in areas of interest. Universities and community colleges offer courses specifically designed for older adults, often at reduced tuition rates or even free. Programs such as Osher Lifelong Learning Institutes (OLLI) provide a wide range of classes on topics like history, literature, science, and current events, without the pressure of exams or grades.

Online Learning Platforms

The rise of online learning platforms has made education more accessible than ever. Websites like Coursera, edX, and Udemy offer courses from renowned institutions that can be taken from the comfort of home. These platforms cover a vast array of subjects, from computer science and business to art and personal development. Retirees can also participate in Massive Open Online Courses (MOOCs) to interact with learners worldwide and join discussion forums to exchange ideas.

Skill Development Workshops

Local community centers, libraries, and senior centers often host workshops on practical skills such as cooking, gardening, digital literacy, and financial management. These workshops provide hands-on learning experiences and opportunities to connect with others who share similar interests. Skill development can also extend to physical activities, with classes available in tai chi, yoga, and other fitness programs designed to improve health and wellness.

Mentorship and Teaching

Many retirees find fulfillment in sharing their knowledge and expertise through mentorship and teaching. Volunteering as a tutor or mentor for students, young professionals, or fellow retirees can be incredibly rewarding. Programs like SCORE (Service Corps of Retired Executives) allow retired business professionals to provide free mentoring to small businesses and entrepreneurs, helping to foster economic growth and innovation.

Creative Pursuits: Art, Music, Writing, and Performing Arts

Engaging in creative pursuits during retirement can be both enjoyable and therapeutic. Art, music, writing, and performing arts offer endless possibilities for self-expression and personal growth, while also fostering community connections.

Visual Arts

Exploring visual arts like painting, drawing, sculpture, and photography can be a deeply satisfying way to spend time. Local art schools, community centers, and galleries often offer classes for beginners and advanced students alike. Participating in art classes not only hones technical skills but also encourages creative thinking and emotional expression.

Painting and Drawing: Whether using watercolors, oils, acrylics, or pencils, painting and drawing allow retirees to capture their perspectives and emotions on canvas or paper.
Sculpture: Working with materials like clay, wood, or metal, sculpture classes offer a tactile and three-dimensional form of artistic expression.
Photography: Digital and traditional photography courses teach composition, lighting, and editing skills, enabling retirees to document their experiences and create stunning visual stories.

Music

Learning to play a musical instrument or joining a choir can provide immense joy and a sense of accomplishment. Music lessons are available for a wide range of instruments, including piano, guitar, violin, and more. Singing in a choir or vocal group not only enhances musical skills but also creates a strong sense of community and shared purpose.

Instrumental Music: Private lessons, group classes, and community bands or orchestras offer opportunities for both beginners and experienced musicians to improve their skills and perform.
Choirs and Vocal Groups: Many community centers and religious organizations host choirs that welcome new members, providing a platform for social interaction and public performance.

Writing

Writing is a powerful medium for self-expression and storytelling. Retirees can explore various forms of writing, including poetry, fiction, memoir, and essays. Writing workshops, both in-person and online, offer structured guidance and feedback from peers and instructors. Participating in a writers' group or attending literary events can also provide inspiration and support.

Fiction and Nonfiction:Creative writing classes help retirees develop their narrative skills, whether crafting novels, short stories, or nonfiction works like memoirs and essays.

Poetry:Poetry workshops encourage participants to experiment with language, form, and rhythm, creating concise and impactful pieces.

Journaling: Keeping a journal can be a reflective practice that enhances self-awareness and captures daily experiences and thoughts.

Performing Arts

The performing arts, including theater, dance, and spoken word, offer dynamic and engaging ways to express creativity. Local theater groups and community centers often provide opportunities for retirees to participate in productions, from acting and directing to set design and stage management.

Theater:Acting classes and community theater productions allow retirees to explore different characters and narratives, enhancing their public speaking and performance skills.

Dance:Dance classes, ranging from ballroom and salsa to contemporary and ballet, offer a fun way to stay active while expressing oneself through movement.

Spoken Word and Storytelling: Participating in spoken word events or storytelling circles enables retirees to share their experiences and perspectives with an audience, fostering a sense of connection and empathy.

Cultivating Connections: Social Clubs, Networking, and Community Engagement

Building and maintaining social connections is vital for a fulfilling retirement. Social clubs, networking opportunities, and community engagement activities provide platforms for retirees to meet new people, share interests, and contribute to their communities.

Social Clubs

Social clubs offer a structured way to meet people with similar interests. These clubs can be centered around hobbies, sports, travel, or cultural activities. Examples include book clubs, gardening clubs, hiking groups, and travel clubs. Many retirement communities and senior centers host these clubs, making it easy to get involved.

Book Clubs:Book clubs provide a space for literary discussion and social interaction. Members read and discuss a variety of books, from fiction and non-fiction to poetry and plays.

Gardening Clubs:Gardening clubs bring together enthusiasts who share tips, plants, and gardening techniques. These clubs often organize garden tours, workshops, and community projects.

Hiking Groups: Hiking groups offer regular opportunities to explore nature and stay fit while enjoying the company of fellow hikers.

Travel Clubs: Travel clubs organize group trips, providing a safe and social way to explore new destinations and cultures.

Networking Opportunities

Even in retirement, networking can be valuable for personal growth and community involvement. Networking events, professional organizations, and alumni associations offer opportunities to connect with others, share experiences, and stay informed about industry developments.

Professional Organizations: Many professional associations offer memberships for retired individuals, allowing them to stay connected with their field and participate in events, conferences, and continuing education.

Alumni Associations: Alumni groups provide a way to reconnect with former classmates, attend reunions, and participate in university events and activities.

Community Networking Events: Local chambers of commerce, business groups, and community organizations often host networking events that welcome retirees looking to engage with local leaders and initiatives.

Community Engagement: Volunteering and community service offer meaningful ways to give back and stay connected. Retirees can choose from a wide range of volunteer opportunities based on their skills and interests.

Local Charities and Nonprofits: Volunteering with local charities and nonprofits allows retirees to support causes they care about, whether it's working at a food bank, mentoring youth, or participating in environmental conservation efforts.

Civic Engagement: Participating in local government, community boards, and neighborhood associations provides a way to influence local policies and improve community well-being.

Educational Support:Retirees can volunteer in schools, libraries, and after-school programs, offering tutoring, reading assistance, and mentorship to students.

In essence, Retirement presents an unparalleled opportunity for lifelong learning, creative pursuits, and community engagement. By pursuing education and skill development, retirees can stay mentally sharp and fulfill their intellectual curiosities. Engaging in creative activities like art, music, writing, and performing arts allows for personal expression and joy. Finally, cultivating social connections through clubs, networking, and community service enhances emotional well-being and fosters a sense of belonging. By integrating these elements into their retirement, individuals can enjoy a vibrant, fulfilling, and enriching chapter of their lives.

7

Unforgettable Experience

Thrill-Seeking Adventures: Skydiving, Hot Air Ballooning, and More

Retirement is often viewed as a time to relax and take things slow, but for many, it represents the perfect opportunity to embark on thrilling adventures and experience life from new, exhilarating perspectives. Engaging in thrill-seeking activities like skydiving, hot air ballooning, and other adrenaline-pumping experiences can infuse retirement with excitement and create unforgettable memories.

Skydiving

Skydiving is the ultimate thrill-seeking adventure, offering an unparalleled sense of freedom and exhilaration. The experience begins with comprehensive training and safety briefings to ensure participants are well-prepared. Tandem jumps, where a novice is securely attached to an experienced instructor, are the most popular option for first-timers. As the plane ascends to an altitude of around 10,000 to 15,000 feet, the anticipation builds. The moment of freefall, lasting approximately 60 seconds, delivers an intense rush as the landscape unfolds below at breathtaking speeds. Once the parachute is deployed, a serene and awe-inspiring descent follows, allowing jumpers to take in panoramic views and savor the experience.

Skydiving is available at various locations worldwide, each offering unique scenery—from coastal views to mountainous terrains. For those who fall in love with the sport, additional training can lead to solo jumps and advanced skydiving techniques.

Hot Air Ballooning

Hot air ballooning provides a more tranquil but equally captivating adventure. This experience allows participants to float gently above the earth, offering a bird's-eye view of the landscape below. The journey typically begins at dawn, as the balloon is inflated and prepared for flight. Once airborne, the sensation of drifting with the wind is both peaceful and exhilarating.

Hot air balloon rides are popular in scenic regions such as Napa Valley, Cappadocia in Turkey, and the Serengeti in Tanzania. Each location offers a unique perspective, whether it's vineyards, ancient rock formations, or vast savannahs teeming with wildlife. The flights usually last about an hour, followed by a traditional champagne toast upon landing—a custom dating back to the earliest balloonists.

Other Thrill-Seeking Adventures

Beyond skydiving and hot air ballooning, there are numerous other adrenaline-fueled activities to explore during retirement:

Bungee Jumping: This extreme sport involves leaping from a bridge or platform while attached to a bungee cord. The freefall and subsequent rebound provide a heart-pounding experience.

Whitewater Rafting: Navigating turbulent river rapids in an inflatable raft offers both thrills and teamwork. Popular destinations include the Colorado River in the USA and the Zambezi River in Africa.

Paragliding: Combining the sensation of flying with the beauty of scenic landscapes, paragliding allows participants to soar through the air, guided by a parachute-like wing.

Scuba Diving: Exploring underwater worlds teeming with marine life provides a sense of adventure and discovery. Destinations like the Great Barrier Reef in Australia and the Blue Hole in Belize are renowned for their diving opportunities.

Once-in-a-Lifetime Events: Attending Concerts, Shows, and Festivals

Retirement offers the freedom to indulge in cultural and entertainment experiences that may have been difficult to fit into a busy work schedule. Attending concerts, shows, and festivals can be incredibly fulfilling, offering a chance to witness world-class performances and immerse oneself in diverse cultural celebrations.

Concerts

Music has the power to evoke emotions and create lasting memories. Attending concerts of favorite artists or discovering new ones can be a highlight of retirement. Major music festivals like Coachella in California, Glastonbury in the UK, and Montreux Jazz Festival in Switzerland draw top talent and offer a wide range of genres. Additionally, intimate performances at local venues provide a closer connection to the music and artists.

For those with specific musical tastes, themed cruises or destination concerts offer unique experiences. For example, classical music enthusiasts might enjoy the Salzburg Festival in Austria, while rock fans could attend the Rock in Rio festival in Brazil.

Shows and Theatrical Performances

The world of theater, ballet, and opera offers countless opportunities for cultural enrichment. Iconic venues like Broadway in New York City, the West End in London, and the Bolshoi Theatre in Moscow host performances that captivate audiences. Retirees can enjoy everything from timeless classics to cutting-edge contemporary productions.

For a unique twist, immersive theater experiences and interactive performances bring the audience into the story, creating a more personal and engaging experience. Cirque du Soleil shows, known for their stunning acrobatics and visual artistry, are also a popular choice for unforgettable entertainment.

Festivals

Festivals are a celebration of culture, community, and creativity. From art and film festivals to food and wine events, there is something for everyone. Some notable festivals include:

Cannes Film Festival (France): A prestigious event showcasing the best in international cinema.
Edinburgh Fringe Festival (Scotland):
The world's largest arts festival, featuring theater, comedy, dance, and music.
Mardi Gras (USA): Known for its vibrant parades and celebrations in New Orleans.
Oktoberfest (Germany): A world-famous beer festival held in Munich, offering a taste of Bavarian culture.

Bucket List Bliss: Achieving Dreams and Fulfilling Goals

Retirement is the perfect time to tackle a bucket list—those dreams and goals that have been set aside for "someday." Whether it's traveling to distant lands, learning new skills, or accomplishing personal milestones, fulfilling bucket list items can bring immense satisfaction and joy.

Traveling to Dream Destinations

Many people dream of visiting iconic destinations around the world. Retirement offers the time and flexibility to plan extended trips and explore places like:

The Great Wall of China: Walking along this ancient marvel provides a sense of history and achievement.
The Pyramids of Egypt: Exploring these ancient wonders offers insight into one of the world's most fascinating civilizations.
Safari in Africa: Witnessing the majestic wildlife in their natural habitat is a life-changing experience.

Learning New Skills

Retirement is an excellent time to acquire new skills and hobbies that were previously put on hold. Whether it's learning a new language, mastering a musical instrument, or taking up painting, the pursuit of new knowledge keeps the mind active and engaged.

Language Learning: Immersing oneself in a new language opens up cultural understanding and enhances travel experiences.
Culinary Skills: Attending cooking classes or culinary schools can transform a love for food into a gourmet adventure.

Craftsmanship: Woodworking, pottery, and other crafts provide both creative outlets and the satisfaction of creating something tangible.

Personal Milestones

Achieving personal milestones can be incredibly rewarding. This could include writing a book, running a marathon, or even participating in volunteer work that makes a significant impact.

Writing a Book: Sharing one's life story, expertise, or creativity through writing can leave a lasting legacy.
Fitness Goals: Completing a marathon, triathlon, or even a long-distance hike like the Appalachian Trail offers a sense of accomplishment and physical vitality.

Volunteer Work: Dedicating time to meaningful causes, such as building homes, teaching, or environmental conservation, provides purpose and fulfillment.

Thrill-seeking adventures, once-in-a-lifetime events, and fulfilling bucket list goals can transform retirement into a period of excitement, discovery, and personal growth. Whether it's skydiving, attending world-renowned festivals, or achieving lifelong dreams, these activities provide rich experiences that enhance the golden years with joy and purpose. Embracing these opportunities ensures that retirement is not just a time of relaxation but a vibrant and fulfilling chapter in life's journey.

Conclusion

Making Every Moment Count: Embracing the Joys of Retirement

Retirement is often seen as the final chapter in the book of life, but it can truly be a vibrant and enriching new beginning. It's a time to rediscover passions, explore new interests, and make the most of the freedom that comes with no longer adhering to a strict work schedule. The key to a fulfilling retirement lies in embracing every moment and finding joy in both the grand adventures and the simple pleasures of daily life.

Rediscovering Passions and Interests

One of the most rewarding aspects of retirement is the opportunity to dive back into passions and hobbies that may have been sidelined during the busy years of a career. Whether it's gardening, painting, playing a musical instrument, or writing, retirement provides the time and mental space to engage deeply in these activities. Rediscovering old hobbies or exploring new ones can bring immense satisfaction and a renewed sense of purpose. Hobbies not only offer a creative outlet but also serve as a means of self-expression and personal fulfillment.

Exploring New Horizons

Retirement is the perfect time to explore new horizons, both literally and figuratively. Travel is a popular pursuit for many retirees, offering the chance to visit new places and experience different cultures. Whether it's embarking on a grand tour of Europe, taking a leisurely road trip across the United States, or exploring the wonders of Asia, travel can enrich the soul and provide countless memorable experiences. Beyond travel, retirement is also a time to try new activities and learn new skills. This could include learning a new language, taking up a sport, or enrolling in classes on subjects ranging from history to technology.

Fostering Connections

Maintaining and fostering connections with family, friends, and the community is crucial for a fulfilling retirement. Social interaction helps combat feelings of loneliness and isolation, which can sometimes accompany this life stage. Joining clubs, participating in group activities, and volunteering are excellent ways to stay socially active. These activities provide opportunities to meet new people, share experiences, and contribute positively to the community. Strong social networks are associated with better mental health and a greater sense of belonging.

Staying Active and Healthy

Physical health is a cornerstone of enjoying retirement to the fullest. Staying active through regular exercise is vital for maintaining strength, flexibility, and overall well-being. Activities such as walking, swimming, yoga, and tai chi are excellent choices for retirees. In addition to physical exercise, mental health should not be overlooked. Engaging in mentally stimulating activities such as puzzles, reading, and learning new skills can help keep the mind sharp. Regular health check-ups and a balanced diet also play significant roles in sustaining good health.

Embracing Simplicity and Mindfulness

In the hustle and bustle of working life, it's easy to overlook the simple joys. Retirement offers a unique opportunity to slow down and appreciate life's small pleasures. Practicing mindfulness and living in the present moment can enhance everyday experiences, making them more meaningful. Whether it's enjoying a cup of coffee on the porch, taking a walk in nature, or spending time with loved ones, these moments of simplicity can bring profound joy and contentment.

Reflecting and Giving Back

Retirement is also a time for reflection and giving back. Reflecting on one's life, achievements, and lessons learned can provide a sense of closure and peace.

Many retirees find fulfillment in giving back to their communities through volunteer work, mentorship, and philanthropy. Sharing knowledge, skills, and time with others can create a lasting positive impact and provide a deep sense of purpose.

As we conclude this exploration of making the most out of retirement, I want to extend my heartfelt thanks to you, the reader, for joining me on this odyssey. Writing this book has been a journey of reflection and discovery, and I hope it has inspired you to embrace the joys of retirement fully. Each chapter has aimed to provide insights, ideas, and encouragement for making this stage of life as enriching and fulfilling as possible.

Your feedback is invaluable to me, and I would greatly appreciate it if you could take a moment to share your honest review of this book. Your thoughts and experiences will not only help me improve but also guide others on their retirement journey.

Remember, retirement is not just an end but a new beginning—a time to make every moment count. Embrace it with joy, curiosity, and an open heart. Here's to a retirement filled with adventures, learning, connections, and, most importantly, happiness.

Thank you, and enjoy every moment of your golden years.